ON BEHALF OF THE PEOPLE

BY RAY CASTLETON

On Behalf of the People

Copyright © Ray Castleton 2017

The moral rights of the author have been asserted.

Cover design © 1889books.co.uk.
Front cover image by Defeye Creative, Chesterfield.
Back cover image courtesy of the Harold White Collection,
National Coal Mining Museum for England

www.1889books.co.uk

ISBN: 978-1-9996440-0-0

To Lynda for all her love and support

On Behalf of The People was commissioned by The National Coal Mining Museum for England to mark the seventieth anniversary of the nationalisation of the coal industry. Four performances of the play produced by The Melting Shop were given at that venue from the 7th to the 9th of June 2017.

The work was then taken on a tour of non-theatre spaces including village halls, workingmen's clubs, miners' welfare halls, community centres etc. The cast for these first performances was as follows:

George	Ray Ashcroft
Connie	Kate Wood
Tom	Adam Horvath
Liz	Lizzie Frain
Director	Charlie Kenber
Movement Director	Patricia Verity Suarez

All set descriptions and stage directions in this version of the text are advisory.

For the 2018 tour, at venues across the North, the part of Tom was played by Danny Mellor, the rest of the cast being the same.

The original performances of the play were staged in the round but can be adapted to suit the size, scale and layout of any venue.

Foreword by Rony Robinson

Nesh?

The war is over. The miner's son returns unexpectedly and dances in the front room with his mother. The father sees them. We're off.

The song they dance to is –

If you were the only girl in the world
And I were the only boy
Nothing else would matter in the world today
We would go on loving in the same old way

From the beginning, we are being asked to ask – will things go on in the same old way? What was the war for, if they do? Whose pits are they going to be? Will it be different between men and women now? Are we going to share things out a bit more?

This Colliery Is Now Being Managed
By The National Coal Board
On Behalf Of the People

On Behalf of The People is a great title for this story about what happens next - including the bitterest ever winter of 1947 (blamed on the miners) –

in the smoky village under the hills and the hawks.

It's about struggle- and not just the union struggle the dad's fought all his life. The family struggles too – which brother was loved most? How do you forgive a father who betrays you and where you come from? How does a father forgive a son who lived when his brother died? Can families survive politics? What if you have to grow up different from your mum and dad? Can a love affair work across picket lines?

There is love everywhere, though it's not usually spoken out loud. Here's the mother talking about her dead son –

He was exactly like you when you were younger... stubborn, biased, inconsiderate, spoke before thinking, and he drank too much.

The play's full of little surprises – often, just when you think you've understood, you haven't. There's a celebration of the language the men use to explain their lives – if their women allow them. And there's a celebration of those women too, and hints of what's coming next for them, forty years on.

You stay here my lad. We need to talk. And if your dad gets up, neither of you are to leave this house before I get back

My favourite scene is when the family have their own private union meeting in their own front room to resolve their own family disputes. I enjoyed the prologue and epilogue's panoramic views of Burnstone lives and history. I admire the long speeches when the people suddenly find their voices.

Should we tear it all down and build something better?

DH Lawrence writes about similar mining families in Sons and Lovers, two world wars earlier, and he asks similar questions (and gives different answers). He isn't always clear whose side he's on, though, even while making great use of our word *nesh*, as if he'd just invented it.

Well, Ray Castleton, writing this new play on behalf of the people, isn't nesh. And we are clear whose side he's on –

The ruling classes are still determined to keep us down. They keep folk poor and blame them for their own poverty, and the working man accepts this shit because he doesn't know any better.

The final speech of the play ends with the good news that –

We're building an industry that'll go on working forever cutting coal on behalf of the people.

But the very last words in the script are then –

The End.

And we remember the song the mother and son danced to at the beginning. And wonder. Can we go on loving – and living – in the same old way?

And should we?

Prologue

Tom This is my town. Burnstone. Where I grew up, where I've come home to.

George Where I work, where I earn our living.

Connie Where I brought up a family, where I made a home.

Liz Where I grew up, where I fell in love, where I wait.

Tom This is my town, Burnstone, a town of two thousand souls every one of them connected to what lays beneath it – coal.

There's been a pit here since 1756 –

George It's not a pit son, that's just a hole in the ground. It's a *mine*, a coal *mine*.

Tom There's been a *mine* here since 1756 – without it there wouldn't be a town. Our lives depend on it.

George It's taken a good few lives an all.

Tom A town on the side of the Pennines.

George On t' reight side of t' Pennines.

Tom In this valley carved out millions of years ago by a raging river, the town grew. First, in the valley bottom, where the shops and the back to back hovels dominate the sides of the slow-flowing, mucky river.

Liz And when the town needed to grow it could only grow upwards. Now the newer grey stone cottages and houses cling to the hillsides as if

	their lives depend on it.
Tom	And at the bottom end of the valley, Burnstone Colliery, its headgear and its winding wheel and its muck heaps dominating the landscape and, some might say, scarring a piece of England's green and pleasant land.
George	Some buggers might say that but it's where we Masons have hewn the coal that's fuelled this nation for four generations.
Connie	And generations of women in this town have struggled against the muck the mine makes to keep their menfolk and their families clean and healthy.
Liz	And some folk escape from here and make a life somewhere else, somewhere nicer – but if you can't escape forever you can always escape for a short while.
Tom	These hills that surround us were made for walking in. Reach the top, see the mucky valley below you, but turn your back on that and the moors spread out in front of you –
Liz	Look at that beautiful view.
Connie	Breathe in that fresh air.
Liz	The town below; like an ugly picture in a beautiful frame. And I'm closer to nature up here than anywhere I've ever been.
George	Look at that hawk soaring and gliding and diving for a kill.
Connie	It's where we had long sunny days, family picnics.

Liz	It's where we held hands, where we made plans.
Connie	My two boys, playing, laughing, running through the fresh, stiff breezes, walking home to wash those faces, red and shiny. Then I'd tuck them both into clean sheets for the best sleep they'd ever had.
Liz	It's where we kissed, where we held each other so tight I thought we'd never let go.
Tom	But I did go. I had to go. Just like millions of other lads all across this globe. Leaving the place they knew, the folks they loved, to fight in places we'd never even heard of.
Liz	I do miss him.
Connie	I hope he's safe.
George	Some never come back.
Tom	But now I am back. Back to Burnstone where the people who love me have waited, back to Burnstone Colliery, where my check and my lamp and my pick and my shovel and the deputy with the snarl and the curse always on his lips, are waiting. They're all waiting. They're waiting for me and the world to get back to normal. After what we've seen, and after what we've done can we ever get back to normal? Or should we tear it all down and build something better?

Act One Scene 1

[It is a Friday afternoon in the late May of 1945

Tom enters. He is in the khaki battle dress uniform of a sergeant in the Yorks and Lancs Regiment. He carries a kit bag.

Connie is busy with her chores. She has her back to him and does not see him. When she turns —]

Connie   Oh my Lord. It's you.

Tom   Well don't sound so disappointed.

Connie   No – I mean why –? Oh! Come here!

[She crosses and embraces him. Holds his face and kisses his cheeks. There are tears. Then she suddenly breaks away.]

You should have let me know. I mean look at me. Look at the state of me. All in my working muck. And look at my hair.

Tom   You always look beautiful to me, Mam.

[He goes to hug her]

Connie   Oh! Get away with your soft soap.

Why didn't you write – we've heard nothing from you for weeks – months.

Tom   But we couldn't –

Connie   I've been beside myself with worry – and Lizzie – she's been here every verse-end, saying: "Any news yet, Mrs Mason?" And I've not known what to tell the girl.

Tom   Listen, Mam, I –

Connie   You've been halfway round the world to – heaven knows where – now you just come

	strolling in without warning –
Tom	We couldn't write, Mam. We weren't allowed to.
Connie	Well, Mrs Bagshaw's had lots of letters from their Terrence.
Tom	Oh aye? Where from?
Connie	Aldershot.
Tom	Aldershot?
Connie	Aye! And Portsmouth!
Tom	Mam, since I was home last I've been to North Africa, crossed the Mediterranean and fought my way through Italy.
Connie	Have you?
Tom	Even we didn't know where we were some days. I didn't receive any letters for ages – mail's still catching up – it can take weeks.
	Last letter I had from my Dad was just after Judd – before I was sent abroad – 'as he sent any since?
Connie	No, you know what he's like.
	How long have you been back in England?
Tom	Since nine o'clock last night. I could have stayed in Portsmouth but I jumped on the first rain I could find. That got me to Derby overnight then I've hitched it the rest of the way.
Connie	You'll be worn out.
Tom	Aye – all that effort to see my beautiful Mam and then all she does is shout at me.
Connie	Your Dad kept saying "No news is good news,

he'll be reight." But –

[She is trying to hold back the tears – Tom recognises her distress He holds her]

Tom	Hey, hey come on, don't be upset. You can see I'm fine.
	I'm here and I'm in one piece. Just about.
Connie	What do you mean *just about*?
Tom	Look, I'm fine. It's just a saying. Like my Dad always says "I'm o'reight up to t' neck!"
	How have you been?
Connie	I've been carrying on – just like everybody else. It's not been easy for anyone.
Tom	And how's my Dad?
Connie	He has good days and bad. But you know what he's like, stubborn as a mule. He's lost weight.
Tom	Has he?
Connie	He's still trying to work as hard ever and he won't have a day off unless he's forced.
Tom	Well, he's always been like that.
Connie	He's putting just as many hours in for the union and the Labour Party.
Tom	He should be slowing down not taking more on.
Connie	He's too proud to do that. I say to him, "What good is your pride when it's making you badly?"
Tom	Aren't lads looking after him?
Connie	Oh yes, but they can't carry him forever. They've all had a try at persuading him to come off the face. It's not pleasing him.

Tom I bet.

Connie And when I tell him it'd be good for his health he keeps reminding me that there'd be a big drop in his money.

But we must count our blessings – compared to some we're lucky. We've a roof over our heads, we've got food on the table – not much of it – but the Lord provides for us, so we're lucky.

Tom You've not changed –

Connie There's people here in Burnstone who've lost all their children…

Tom I know.

Come on, Mam. Come on. Hey, here let's dry your eyes.

Connie I'm sorry, Tommy.

Tom Hey! You don't have to say sorry to me, Mam. You never have to say sorry to me.

Hey, nar then, I almost forgot. I've got you something.

[He goes to his kit bag]

Connie What do you mean?

Tom *[Rummaging in bag]*

Hang on, I'm trying to find it.

[He pulls something from the bag, stands and hides it behind his back.]

Tom Close your eyes and hold your hands out.

Connie Don't be so daft!

Tom Come on, or there's no surprise.

[Connie does as he bids but Tom takes his time, teasing her.]

Tom   Keep them eyes shut.

Connie   You silly thing. What are you doing?

Tom   No peeping.

Connie   I'm not!

[He places a silk scarf across her outstretched hands. She opens her eyes.]

Oh Tommy, it's beautiful. Look at the colours. It's real silk. It must have cost you a fortune. Ooh, I daren't wear this out in the street –

Tom   Don't be silly, Mam. You've as much right to wear nice things as anybody.

Connie   It must have cost you a pretty penny. Where did you get it?

Tom   Italy – it cost a packet. But you're worth it.

Connie   Oh Tommy!

Tom   Well come on then – don't just sit there looking at it, get it tried on.

[She drapes the scarf around her shoulders.]

Tom   Wow! Mam, you look beautiful. Wait 'til Dad sees you in that. He'll be taking you out dancing.

Connie   Nay lad, our dancing days are over.

Tom   Never. Come here.

Connie   You daft thing – what do you think you're doing?

Tom   May I have this dance, Madame?

[She has no choice. He waltzes her around the space singing as they go. She is laughing in spite of herself]

Tom *[sings]* If you were the only girl in the world
And I were the only boy,
Nothing else would matter in the world today,
We could go on loving in the same old way.

[George enters in his pit clothes and stands watching. Connie and Tom suddenly see him and stop dancing]

Act One Scene 2

[The same]

George So you're back then? Have they run out of pencils and paper in the army?

Connie He's been telling me, George, they weren't allowed to write.

George Oh aye? Your Mam's been worried sick about you.

Tom We weren't allowed to in case we might give summat away.

George Oh aye?

Tom Anyway how are you? Mam says you've not been so good.

[He holds out his hand to his father who shakes it, but it lacks Connie's earlier enthusiasm.]

George I'm o'reight up to t' neck.

I see tha's got three stripes up. They must be running out of blokes to pick from if tha's been made up to Sergeant.

Tom Oh aye, they're having to scrape the barrel.

George So, when are you going back?

Connie Don't ask him that. He's only just walked through the door and you're asking him when he's going back.

George When you've got that uniform on you're at their beck and call.

Tom I've just got three days leave, Dad.

Connie	Three days! Is that all?
Tom	We've all to report to battalion HQ in Sheffield on Monday.
Connie	Monday?
Tom	Some of the lads have not even travelled up yet. We docked in Pompey and they told us we could have a four-day pass; some of 'em haven't even bothered going home. They've stayed there until Sunday on a bender.
George	I don't blame 'em!
Connie	But what happens then? Where might they send you? When will you be demobbed?
George	Bloody hell, Connie, slow down. Give the lad a chance to answer one question before tha asks bloody next 'un.
Connie	Language!
Tom	Well, what they've told us is that we report back and then talk about who's staying in and who wants to get out.
Connie	Well, they don't need to ask you that question, do they?
George	He's still got to do as he's told and go back though. If he's like I was after t' first lot he'll not be able to get out bloody fast enough.
Tom	*[Changing subject]* Hey, what do you think to my Mam's present, Dad? Doesn't she look a picture?
George	Tha'd best not wear that to Chapel on Sunday. They'll be chucking thi out as a bloody Jezebel.

Connie   You see, Tommy: he's not changed a bit. He's just as rude, blasphemous and sarcastic as ever.

Tom   Well I think you look grand. "Lady Constance Mason, The Duchess of Burnstone!"

Anyway, Dad I've got something for you an' all.

[He goes to his kit bag and begins to rummage.]

George   Tha shouldn't have bothered. There's nowt I need.

Tom   *[Handing him a small tissue paper parcel]* Here you are. I hope you like it.

[George stares at the package but makes no effort to open it]

George   What is it?

Connie   Well if you open it you'll happen find out won't you!

[He still hesitates.]

Well go on then! You might not want to know what t' lad's brought you but the suspense is killing me.

George   All right, don't rush me.

[He removes the paper slowly to reveal a leather wallet. He looks at it and says nothing.]

Tom   Do you like it, Dad?

[George is about to answer when –]

Connie   Of course he does. Well, George, say something to the lad.

George   Has tha put owt in it?

Connie   George! You ungrateful old –

Tom   I know what he means, Mam. When you give

	somebody a wallet you're supposed to put money in to bring good luck.
George	Well has tha?
Tom	Have a look. *[George looks inside.]*
George	Ten bob.
Connie	Oh! Tom that's too much.
George	Nay it isn't. It's not a bad sneck lifter is that.
Tom	Aye, I've only put it in so you can treat me to a pint in the Lion tonight.
George	I will –
Connie	You will if you're well enough –
George	I'll feel better when I've got some grub inside me. Has tha got dinner on?
Connie	You'll have to wait.
George	Why?
Connie	Well for one thing you're early again and for another, now our Tommy's turned up I'll need to do extra –

[During the following, she fetches her coat and puts it on]

	– So I'm going to see if Jack Parkin's got any meat left.
George	Tha'll be lucky at this time. It's half past three. They've had nowt left by ten o'clock some mornings.
Connie	Well if I don't try I'll never know will I? Chalky brought me some veg up from the allotment this morning so we'll be all right for greens.

[She turns to go, stops, then turns back.]

>Instead of sitting there with a face like thunder why don't you get washed, get changed in to summat decent and make your lad a cup of tea.

Tom It's all right, Mam, I'll make it.

[He gets up and goes to the range at the back. Connie gives George a look and exits.]

Act One Scene 3

[The same. A few minutes later]

Tom Here we are. *[He turns as he puts tea things on the table.]*

George Tha's not forgotten how to make tea then?

Tom Nay, Dad, it didn't matter where we were, or how bad things got, there were always a cuppa on the go.

How's things at work then?

George Bloody awful.

Tom Oh.

George Well, there's not enough manpower for a start. Not since the minute they blew the bugle and all you lads buggered off.

Tom So what have they done about it?

George Some of the ideas they've come up with have been bloody daft.

Tom How do you mean?

George Well, Ernie Bevin's come up with this scheme. He's drafted in these lads of his, Bevin's Boys they're calling 'em, but they're all but useless. No more than kids and never done a proper days work in their lives. And when you've got 'em underground they're a bloody liability. They're not bloody safe.

Tom You used to say that about me when I started.

George Nay this is different. Tha were from mining

	stock so tha did have bit of knowledge about job, these buggers haven't a clue. Thank God lads like thee are coming back.
	I mean give 'em their due, the government's finally invested in some new cutting machines. Not before time. Seeing as we've been asking the bloody board of directors for 'em since 1933. Productivity is up a bit now. Lads are earning a bit more.
Tom	That's better for you then.
George	New machines make too much dust.
Tom	Aye, Mam said you were struggling to cope.
George	Oh, did she now?
Tom	Dad – don't you think you've done your stint on t' face? Shouldn't you be thinking of coming off?
George	Don't you bloody start. What with your Mam and t' lads at work on at me –
Tom	They're just trying to do their best for you –
George	I'm o'reight as I am. Anyway, I've too much on, apart from work. There's union – Labour Party – we've got an election to win in June tha knows. And I've still to earn our keep – no bugger else will.
Tom	Dad, I need to talk to you about our Judd –
George	Nay, no amount of talking's going to bring him back –
Tom	I know that – but I need to put things straight between us –

George   You're wasting your time, lad.

Tom   But I want you to know how it was –

George   I know how it was, Tom.

Tom   We had to go, Dad –

George   I've told thee – there's no more to be said. What's been done can't be undone.

Tom   Dad –

George   It can't be undone with a cosy cup o' tea and a chat at side a t' fire. I'm going for a wash.

[George gets up and crosses.]

Tom   Dad, I want it sorting out now. *[Tom stops him with a hand on his chest. George looks at the hand and then into Tom's eyes.]*

George   Don't you bloody dare –

[Tom breaks away.]

[Blackout]

Act One Scene 4

[It is the park, the same day, early evening. There is a bench. Liz waits pacing impatiently. She keeps glancing in the direction from which she expects to see Tom appear. As she turns away from it he appears behind her.]

Tom	Liz.
Liz	You made me jump.
Tom	Sorry – you got my note then.
Liz	Yes. A bit brief, "Meet me at five at the old place in the park."
	It was a bit of a shock – why didn't you let anybody know you were coming?
Tom	We weren't allowed to write because –
Liz	Did you get my letters?
Tom	Some of them –
Liz	Was it awful?
Tom	Sometimes.
Liz	I bet you're glad it's over.
Tom	Aye.
Liz	It's good to have you back – I've missed you.
	How long are you home for?
Tom	Until Monday.
Liz	Only three days?
Tom	I've got to report to Battalion HQ in Sheffield to find out what happens next.

Liz	So you'll be close by?
Tom	Oh Aye, I'll be close by.
Liz	I – I thought you'd been killed.
Tom	Shush. Don't say that.
Liz	I did though. I thought I'd go round to your Mam's one day and see her sat there with the telegram on the table –
Tom	Don't –
Liz	I've been round every day to see if she'd had word. I must have driven her barmy.
Tom	She doesn't mind. She likes you.
Liz	Your Dad doesn't. He was sick of the sight of me.
Tom	Aye well – that's my Dad for you –
Liz	Yeah – I err – you know – err –
Tom	What?
Liz	No, I can't –
Tom	Go on, you've started now.
Liz	Well, you know when – oh, this is going to sound awful.
Tom	Go on.
Liz	Well when I heard what had happened to Judd – I was sad just like everybody else but –part of me – a big part of me – was saying – I'm glad it's not Tom.

Does that sound awful?

I mean if it hadn't have been for what happened |

to you it could have been you going on to that beach and –

[Tom turns from her.]

Liz	I'm sorry – I've missed you. I've missed your letters.
Tom	I keep telling people it was difficult to write.
Liz	Wouldn't they let you?
Tom	Sometimes they wouldn't.
Liz	Sometimes?
Tom	Well, most of the time. And most of the time you had a gun in your hand so you had no time for a pencil.
	And even if you did find time, you didn't know what to write – what to say.
Liz	You didn't know what to say – to me?
Tom	Didn't know what to say to anybody – it's hard to explain, sorry.
	I had a job to track you down today. I went to Webster's and they told me you'd left.
Liz	Got sick of factory work.
Tom	I never thought I'd see you working at the pit.
Liz	Me neither, but it's not just colliers they've lost, – its clerical staff as well. Anyway, a pit office is better than a factory – it's cleaner – and I'm learning a lot.
Tom	Learning?
Liz	Shorthand and typing.
Tom	That's a big change from bottling pickles.

Liz You know, I never thought I could do it, but the teacher at college says I'm doing well.

Tom College?

Liz Well, that sounds posh. It's night school really. I go over to Barnfield after work on the bus two nights a week.

Tom Listen to you – college girl!

Liz Don't mock. A lot of people round here mock when you're trying to better yourself. Don't you be one of them.

Tom Keep your hair on, I was only joking.

Liz Well I've heard enough of it, especially from my Mam. "Don't you get ideas above your station our Elizabeth – know your place."–Well the last few years have changed all that. Even round here. Nobody knows what their place is any more.

Tom How do you mean?

Liz You know my Mam's sister, Edna, the one who lives in Sheffield –

Tom No.

Liz You do, little woman – talks a lot!

Tom Oh aye –

Liz Well her husband, my Uncle John, went off to war. Next I hear my Auntie Edna's working in the steel works – as a crane driver – in the furnaces where he used to work. My Mam's going to see her tomorrow, Auntie Edna's got the weekend off.

	It's the first time my mam's been brave enough to go to Sheffield since the Blitz. Err – she's taking our Norman with her.
	So – all day tomorrow – I've got the house to myself.
Tom	Right.
Liz	I was supposed to be going with her but now you're back…
Tom	When is she going?
Liz	Eight o'clock train.
Tom	Are you inviting me round for my dinner then?
Liz	If you like. Say twelve o'clock?
Tom	Well, I'll have to check my diary. I'm not sure if I can make it.
Liz	You'd better –
Tom	Or what?
Liz	Or I'll come and find you.
Tom	I'll be there for half eleven.
Liz	Hey, what time is it now?
Tom	Twenty to six.
Liz	I need to go home.
Tom	What, already?
Liz	My mam expected me an hour ago. She'll be wondering where I've got to.
Tom	Can't you stop a bit longer – because I don't want to go back yet?
Liz	I promised to help her get ready – you

	remember what she was like.
Tom	Aye.
Liz	Well she's got worse. She'll be panicking. Will I see you later?
Tom	Yes. I'll come round – call for you –
Liz	Right – see you later then.

[They kiss and embrace then she breaks away.]

I've got to go.

[She starts to go]

Tom	Liz.
Liz	Yes?
Tom	I've got something to ask you.
Liz	Yes?

[He hesitates.]

Tom	Well I err, – I'm taking my Dad to the Yellow Lion tonight. Will you come?
Liz	Is that all?
Tom	Yes.
Liz	Of course I will – see you later.

[She leaves and Tom is alone. He sits.]

Act One Scene 5

[The Masons' kitchen later that evening. Tom Enters.]

Tom Where's my Dad?

Connie He's upstairs having a nap. He said you and him had a row.

Tom Not exactly.

Connie Well what would you call it then?

Tom There's two sides to a row, Mam. It's only a row when both people talk – he wouldn't.

Connie He wouldn't talk about Judd, you mean?

Tom No.

Connie But he will, in time.

Tom I need to get it out in the open, now, Mam –

Connie I've told you he's still grieving – but he'll come round –

Tom What about you though, Mam? He was the apple of your eye an' all –

Connie You both were! There's never been a favourite in this house!

I've told him – the Lord's taken him and no amount of anger or blame will ever bring him home to me – to us.

Tom But he's just avoiding it.

Connie You know what he's like at the best of times, stubborn as a mule.

Tom That's just it though in't it – he's not like this.

	Not when it comes to voicing an opinion on owt else. When I asked him about work and union he was t' same as ever, he could talk hind leg off a donkey.
Connie	Yes but this is different. It's hit him hard.
Tom	I know he was always Dad's favourite.
Connie	Don't say that. There's never been –
Tom	It's true, Mam.

[Connie looks down and shakes her head.]

Connie	You've got to give him time love.
Tom	I haven't got time, Mam. I need to make decisions and I need to make 'em now.
Connie	What decisions?
Tom	Whether to come home or to stay in.
Connie	What do you mean?
Tom	Look, Mam – I can't come back if my Dad don't want me here.

[Tom takes a manila envelope and a scrap of paper from his pocket.]

Tom	A little lad brought this. There's a note.
Connie	*[Reads the note]* Oh – I can't go – not tonight – we've got some sorting out to do here.
Tom	Don't worry, Mam. As soon as Dad gets up I'll talk to him then take him for that pint.
Connie	There'll be no trips to the Lion tonight, Tom. Not after what you've just told me – I've lost one son forever – then the other one no sooner comes back and he's talking about going away.

[She gets her coat.]

Tom Where are you going now?

Connie To Ada Slater's. She won't say boo to a goose normally. But she can give this report to the WVS tonight. It's all written down for her – so she's got no excuse – she can read.

You stay here my lad. We need to talk. And if your Dad gets up, neither of you are to leave this house before I get back.

Do you hear?

Tom Aye.

[Connie goes]

Act One Scene 6

[The Mason's kitchen thirty minutes later, George has just come downstairs. He sits in his chair reading his paper. Tom sits at the table sorting out his kit bag. There is a long silence. George looks towards the outside door. Tom watches him. Connie enters.]

Connie Right.

[She takes her coat off and means business]

Now then, George put that paper down and come to this table. We all need to talk – properly.

George Nowt's changed in t' last three hours.

Connie It's got to be discussed, properly.

[George ignores her.]

Connie In all the years I've known you you've never turned your back on a problem, have you?

George No.

Connie Well this problem needs discussing, now.

George I've told thee, it'll make no difference.

Connie George, come to this table and listen to the lad.

Tom What was it you always taught me? Make the other bloke understand your position.

George That's when its union business, for disputes –

Connie This is a *dispute*. And it's more important than any of your union work. Now get to this table, stop being so stubborn and listen?

[George puts his paper down. And moves reluctantly to the table]

George Go on then – say thi piece.

Tom I know our Judd was always your favourite –

Connie I've told you there was no favourites in this house–

Tom It's all right, Mam. What I'm trying to say, Dad – I understand how you must feel about our Judd – but I didn't make him join up and –

George But if it hadn't been for thee going –

Connie Hold on, George. Tom's still in the chair. He's still explaining his "position".

[She indicates that he must continue.]

Tom You know as well as I do that our Judd never asked anybody's opinion on owt, and he certainly never asked mine on that.

He just came back that day and said, "Next Thursday." I said, "What tha on about 'Next Thursday'?" He said, "I've joined your mob, reporting for duty next Thursday." I told him you'd go barmy –

Connie And you did.

Tom Our Judd just laughed – he said: "I can't have my little brother showing me up can I? And I don't want folk round here calling me a coward."

But really, he wanted to go for the same reasons as me. Because of what you've always taught us.

George And what's that?

Tom That if we saw summat worth fighting for, or against, we should do it. Well as I saw it – and I still do – Jerry were taking over every country in

	Europe – we had to stop him because we were going to be next. I had to go, and our Judd felt he had to go. War changes everything, Dad.
George	I know that, I don't need thee to tell me that.

[To Connie]

	Oh, sorry, Connie, can I have the bloody chair now please?
Connie	Yes, but moderate your language.
George	Right, well, let me tell you summat now.
	They asked us to fight for king and country in 1915. Waved us off and told us we were brave lads. One hundred and forty-seven lads from this little town alone didn't come back. Good men. Miners most on 'em. Lads I'd worked with, cheek by jowl.
	And those of us who were lucky enough to come back were promised the earth. But they rewarded us by treating no better than the shit they scraped off their boots.
Connie	George!
George	You know what I mean, Connie. You lived through it all with me and you know that they treated us as if we were summat to be chucked away. Didn't they?
Connie	Aye.
George	Not needed any more. Then twenty years later they ask miners like thee and Judd to fight for king and country – again. Can you blame me for wanting to stop you and him from going?
Tom	That was a different time. We've been fighting

	for a different cause. A just cause.
George	Oh aye. Maybe. But I'll tell thee one thing that was exactly the same. They told you that if you didn't go you'd be branded as a traitor or a coward, just like we were told twenty-odd years before – like you told him –
Tom	I didn't tell him he'd be –
George	And if tha hadn't have shamed him into going I could have talked him into staying.
Tom	I never told him he was a coward.
George	And he wasn't. Ask any bugger. He got stuck in – did his stint, he were a proper union man, stood up to the bosses for his mates as well as himself.
Connie	We know that, George but –
George	We can't afford to lose men like him – especially now –
Connie	What does that mean?
George	It's going to be a different world, Connie. We need strong union lads like our Judd – our Tom's never been interested.
Tom	Of course I have – I've always been a union man – only I've never stood on a soap-box made a noise about it.
	And when I come back home, if I come back home, I'll come back as Tom Mason not as a replacement for Judd Mason.
George	Aye, but will tha be up to it?
Tom	The trouble is whatever I do it'll never be good

enough for you will it? Because I'm not Judd.

[He fetches his tunic.]

Connie Don't go out, love! Where are you going?

Tom I'm not going anywhere, Mam. I'm showing my Dad something.

You see these? *[His stripes]* Eh? When you first came in and saw that I'd been made up to sergeant you didn't give me an ounce of credit for it. You joked about it. Well, I've earned these stripes, Dad.

My officers saw how I looked after my mates and how they listened to me. How I helped 'em when we were in a jam. They asked me what I'd done in Civvy Street and I told them I'd been a miner that I'd worked underground alongside my Dad. And I was proud to tell 'em that. And I told 'em that he's a union delegate and he's taught me everything I know. About looking after the people who work with me, about sticking together, because if you don't, men's lives are at risk. That's what got me these.

George I see – is that it.

Tom When I heard the news about our Judd dying in Normandy I was still in hospital. If I hadn't have had that bloody ruptured appendix, I'd have been on one of those boats going over with my company, just like our Judd did with his.

George We know all that.

Tom What you don't know, Dad, is that I think about that every waking minute –

Over the last five years I've seen things and

	done things that nobody should ever have to see or do – terrible things. But what stops me sleeping at night is nowt to do with any of that. It's thinking it should have been me instead of our Judd –
Connie	Don't say that, Tom.
Tom	I try not to think about it every day, Mam. *[To George]* But the words in that letter about you not being able to forgive me for my own brother's death have hurt me more than any bloody bullet or shell –
	I'm sorry, Mam I didn't want to say all that in front of you, but I know it's the only way I'll ever get him to listen.
	I don't think I can't put up with it like this, Dad. I can't come back if you're going to go on resenting me as much as this.
	They've told me I could have a good career in the army. I've got until Monday to decide. *[He goes.]*

Act One Scene 7

[There is a long silence during which Connie stares at George. To avoid her stare, he goes and sits in his chair.]

Connie   How dare you? Eh, how have you got the gall?

George   What?

Connie   So, you're not mourning the loss of a son, it's the loss of a good "union man"?

George   It's both.

Connie   These last few months I've watched you and I've had nothing but love and pity in my heart for you. I've sat with you and cried with you and listened to you telling me over and over about the son you've lost. The son who was precious to you and was a part of you –

George   And I meant every bloody word.

Connie   I'm sure you did, but you never said the main reason for missing him was because of the union – your *bloody* politics. And your other son's come back from the other side of hell, just like you once did, and all you do is shun him. Treat him like a leper in his own home.

George   That's not what I'm doing.

Connie   Oh, but it is, and you should hang your head in shame, George Mason.

George   That's not bloody fair, Connie – and it's not what I said. We need young blood who'll fight as hard as we did.

Connie   And don't you think our Tommy'll do that?

George No I don't.

Connie Why – because he's not like you? Because he's not like Judd?

George It's not that –

Connie It is! You always favoured Judd over Tommy because he was your double. And not just in looks.

George What do you mean?

Connie He had all your faults as well. And, God forgive me, I'm speaking ill of the dead here. But he was exactly like you when you were younger.

George What's wrong with that?

Connie Stubborn, biased, inconsiderate, spoke before thinking and he drank too much.

George Bloody hell, Connie, don't pull any punches will you.

Connie You know it's true. He wasn't the hero you saw him as. But he was like you used to be. You were full of life and energy and believed you could take on the world and everybody in it.

And that's why I loved you.

And it's why I loved our Judd, in spite of all the trouble he brought home.

George That were nowt –

Connie And I know it's why you thought so much about him. You could see yourself in him thirty years ago.

George He should never have gone, Connie.

Connie But he did go. You didn't want him to go.

	Neither did I. But Tommy's right, do you think that once he'd made his decision to go anybody could have stopped him.
George	I do miss him.
Connie	I know love, so do I, so does Tommy. And this house will be' empty without him stamping about and making his racket. But nothing any of us can do is ever going to bring him home.

You've lost the son that you saw as carrying on where you'll be leaving off. Well, you can't think that way. You can't re-live your past through your children. They find their own way and it'll be different to your way because times have changed. |
| **George** | We've got to make sure that they go on changing for the better. |
| **Connie** | And Tommy and all the lads coming home will want that too. But, like he says, he's got do it his way – not your way or Judd's way – because he's his own man now. He's all grown up into a fine young man and I'm proud of him. And you should be too, not blaming him for something he didn't do. |

Act One Scene 8

[It is the snug of the Yellow Lion Pub. There is the noise of a busy pub but as if it is coming from another room. Tom and Liz walk in with drinks and sit at a table.]

Liz   It's a bit quieter in here.

Tom   Yes, but we can hear ourselves think.

Liz   Everybody was pleased to see you back.

Tom   Aye, it's nice to know. If I take every pint I've been offered in there you'll have to carry me home.

Liz   I hope you're not expecting me to do that in the future, Mr Mason.

Tom   Only now and again – or possibly every Friday night.

Liz   You still make me laugh, I'll be glad when your home for good.

Tom   I bumped in to John Harris on t' way here. I hear you've been having a nice time without me.

Liz   How do you mean?

Tom   Dancing, pictures –

Liz   Only now and again –

Tom   Only dancing every week.

Liz   Yes, but –

Tom   And the pictures "occasionally." And with lads an' all.

Liz   I go out along with about a dozen or more other

	lads and lasses. But I've never been out with a bloke on my own. And if you don't believe me you can ask 'em. You know all of 'em anyway.
Liz	Tom Mason, you're not jealous are you?

[Tom does not answer.]

	You are aren't you? Well, you've no need to be. I've waited for you for five years.
Tom	I don't believe you.
Liz	It's true.
Tom	You'll have to prove it to me.
Liz	How?
Tom	When I come round for dinner tomorrow.
Liz	You cheeky – *[they kiss]*
	When you're home for good I'll prove it to you every day.
Tom	Liz, I've got something to ask you.
Liz	Yes –
	Well go on.
Tom	Well – it's not easy to explain.
Liz	I think you need to try –
Tom	No, it's not that –
Liz	Hey, It's not about me going out is it? Because –
Tom	No, I was only pulling your leg –
Liz	Well what is it?
Tom	Well you know my Dad's always said it was my fault that our Judd joined up.

Liz   That's silly.

Tom   Well – just before my posting abroad he sent me a letter – blaming me –

Liz   That's a terrible thing to do.

Tom   I can't live here –

Liz   What do you mean?

Tom   I can't come home, seeing him every day, knowing that.

Liz   But, we could get somewhere else to live – you and me – it doesn't mean you have to leave Burnstone –

Tom   But, I'd still see him –

Liz   Where would you go? What would you do?

Tom   That's what I wanted to ask you. They say I can stay in the army. My officers are keen on it. They say I can make a career of it.

Liz   I'm sure *you* can, – but where does that leave me? Where does it leave *us*?

Tom   You could come with me. They have married quarters. I'd be home every night. Well, I would if I got a home posting. It'd just be like having a normal job.

Liz   And what about my job?

Tom   Well, you'd have to give it up if we got married anyway –

Liz   You don't understand, do you? I'm the breadwinner in our house. Since my Dad left. My mam and our Norman rely on me. I can't just up sticks and go.

And what if you had to go abroad again? The war's not over in the Far East yet. Some lads from Burnstone are still out there. How long will that last? And then – what if there's another war?

[Pause]

Tom I need to tell 'em on Monday.

Liz Well, tell 'em they'll have to wait.

Tom Liz –

Liz If that was a proposal it's not the kind I'd been expecting. I'm not sure that's the life I'd want.

[George enters]

Tom Dad!

George Err – I'm not stopping long – I'm on earlies in the morning.

[He takes out his new wallet and takes out the ten-bob note.]

I've just come in for a quick half and to treat my son and his lady friend to a drink.

[He holds out his hand to Tom who shakes it.]

Act One Scene 9

[Liz's house a few hours later.]

Tom I'm sorry.

Liz What is it?

Tom It were just a bad dream –

Liz You screamed out – look at you you're sweating.

Tom Sorry.

Liz It's all right.

Tom It's just sometimes you wake up and you forget where you are.

Liz You can always tell me you know – whatever it is.

Tom No – *[She holds him.]*

Liz It's all right. Most people think war's like they see at the pictures – I know it's not.
What is it?
Tell me.

Tom I can't.

Liz Tell me.

Tom Once we had to clear these woods – Germans were using them as cover – it'd gone on for days – we couldn't go in and we couldn't go round the forest – it were too far – so they burnt 'em out – flame throwers – I'd seen a lot by then, but nowt like that. All the forest – it'd been beautiful – reduced to ashes.

Anyway, it broke their cover all right – ones who got out alive soon surrendered and we could march on.

One of my officers sent me into the field hospital to get a report – I wanted to go anyway – some of the lads from my platoon had been hit – so I wanted to make sure they were all right.

As I looked round this big tent, I could see there were about forty or fifty blokes all with different wounds – I could stomach it – after what we'd seen before – it didn't upset me.

But the worse thing in there was a smell – like burnt meat – I'd never smelled anything like it. At the other end of this tent – away from our lads somebody was calling out – I got up and went to see what it was. As I got closer I could see this body – you could tell it was a body but, only just – that many burns. It was him who was making the noise.

As I got closer I could hear what he was trying to say – he was trying to talk through the pain – "mutter – mutter" – he kept saying.

At the side of his bed was his dog tag – I suppose it was the only thing on him that hadn't burned – it said his name, rank and number – it had his date of birth – 1929 – he was fifteen.

In his pain he grabbed hold of my hand – he kept squeezing it – as best he could anyway – and all the time he was saying in German – "mutter – mutter."

One of the nurses came over – to see what I was doing I think. When she saw she just smiled and – I'll never forget it – she just smiled and nodded – then she walked away.

I got this pillow off another bed and I held it over his face – I just held it there until he stopped breathing – no more breath – no more "mutters".

I got up to go back – that same nurse was seeing to someone else by now. I walked past her and back to my mate's bedside.

I watched her. She went to the German lad and covered him and his face with a clean white sheet.

No more pain – no more "mutters."

It's hard to hate a whole nation of people once you've seen something like that.

Act One Scene 10

[The Masons' kitchen, Sunday night, Tom's kit bag is almost packed.]

Connie I hope he's got everything –

George Gi' o'er fussing –

Connie I don't want him missing anything –

George That's umpteenth time tha's said that – he's only going to Sheffield.

[Tom enters with some of his stuff and packs it into his bag.]

Connie Now, are sure you've got everything?

Tom Yes, Mam.

Connie I hope so. Mind you, at least you'll not be far away this time. You can always come back for stuff – or we can bring it to you.

George Give over fussing, Connie. He knows what he's doing. What time are you leaving, Tom?

Tom The best trains at seven. I'll be at HQ for nine.

George Aye if they're running right. Tha knows what trains are like.

Are tha all right for cash?

Tom Dad – course I am. You don't have to –

George I know but –

Tom Listen, I got some back-pay in Pompey when we docked, and I'll get some more tomorrow.

George That's all right then, no lad of mine's ever gone short.

Connie When will you be home again?

Tom I'm not sure, Mam – but at least for a few weeks I'm only going to be a train ride away.

Connie When will you be demobbed?

George Stop asking bloody silly questions, Connie –

Tom I'm not sure, Mam – but I'll be home as soon as they'll let me out.

Connie Well, you must tell them that you've got good reasons to come home.

Tom I will that, Mam. I'll do my best.

Err – listen, I told Liz I'd pop round and see her tonight. I won't get a chance in the morning – she'll be at work – I won't be back late.

Connie Oh aye, of course, you must go –

George I shall happen be in bed when tha gets back – and I shan't see thi tomorrow morning – so I'll say cheerio now.

If tha can get back anytime for a day or two's leave – it'd be grand.

[Connie and Tom exchange satisfied glances at the reconciliation.]

Then tha can come out with me and t' lads canvassing for the party, we need as many hands as we can.

Connie You don't need to canvass round here – you could stick a Labour rosette on a monkey it'd get elected.

George Not round here. We're going over to Millsley to get the bloody Tories out.

Tom I'll do what I can, Dad. I'll be seeing you – soon.

[Tom Goes]

Act One Scene 11

[The streets of Millsley, Mid-June, 1945.

We see all our characters wearing red rosettes handing out election literature to passers-by, occasionally door knocking and reacting to the various responses from the constituents.]

Act One Scene 12

[Late June 1945
It is a crowded meeting in the town hall of the marginal constituency of Millsley. George sits at the back of the platform with Connie nervously waiting his turn to speak.]

George I'm not sure this is a good idea, Connie.

Connie I've told you, you'll be fine.

George I don't know so much.

Connie If Charles Darlow hadn't had the confidence in you, he wouldn't have asked you to speak on his behalf, would he?

George Aye but he's only heard me speak to union men before. These buggers here are all bloody Tories.

Connie Just remember where you are and moderate your language.

George I've not said a bloody word –

Connie Sshhhhh

[George starts to read self-consciously from a written note.]

George Thank you for your warm welcome Ladies and Gentlemen.

　　　　　I've been asked here tonight to support Mr Charles Darlow as your Labour party candidate for the forthcoming General Election. And I am proud and honoured to do that as I have known Mr Darlow for many years. I know that this is traditionally a Conservative seat but there are sweeping changes needed across our country… I … I …

[He stops and looks at the audience.]

> Look, err – I'm sorry – I wrote that down before I came because I was nervous about speaking here tonight – it's all true like –
>
> Charlie is good bloke – but this – well it's not really me speaking. You see I'm used to speaking with no punches pulled to miners, union lads and their bosses, men who speak like I do – plain and straightforward.

[He looks at Connie.]

> Sometimes I'm a bit too plain and straightforward for my wife's liking.

[He looks at Connie again. She shakes her head.]

> After t' Great War, through the two decades that followed it, they told us, "There's not much demand for coal".
>
> And some days I'd turn up at the colliery and they didn't even give me a shift – that meant no pay, no bread on the table, no rent money. If there was any work at all, they gave us what shi– err, what awful jobs they could – and paid us a bloody pittance for doing 'em. And if we complained they told us to get on with it because we were lucky to have a job at all.
>
> And if you complained too much they'd send you home wi' nowt.
>
> "If you don't like it get off to the labour exchange, cap in bloody hand."
>
> But then along comes another war and they suddenly recognise you. They suddenly see that maybe we do have a value. Perhaps this ignorant, dirty, working man *is* needed. So, they

tell us that they need as much coal as possible to help the war effort, to help save the nation. And suddenly there are extra shifts and extra rations for us. And suddenly the government can find the money to buy the machines and to provide the conditions we've been asking for t' past twenty years.

And my union members are not complaining because their wages are better than they've ever been. And the bloody management and the owners and the shareholders have had a very good war, thank you very much.

Meanwhile, while they've all got their noses in the capitalist trough, lads like my sons, and I'm sure some of your sons, are not being given work, they're been given a bloody uniform and a gun and sent off to fight against another nation's young men and boys, to slaughter each other because prime ministers and Kings can't find better ways to solve problems.

Now, I know that after what we've all been through, what I've just said might not sound very patriotic. But let me tell you: I'm the last person to disrespect those lads.

My eldest son is lying in a grave in Normandy – a grave that I'll probably never get to see.

And that's why I'm working so hard to get a government elected that'll look after these lads who've come home. Like my youngest boy who, after risking his neck to serve his country is coming home, to serve it again in the mining industry.

I want a government with the will to look after

him and all the working classes who have always been the backbone and muscle of this country in times of crisis.

Because if you vote for a party that'll do that you'll be voting for a party that's going to rebuild your country with fairness and justice.

For a change.

Act One Scene 13

[The Masons' kitchen 26 July 1945
Connie is busy with chores when Tom bursts in. He is in his working clothes.]

Tom Mam, Mam, have you heard the news?

Connie Shush! With your shouting and bawling –

Tom Where's my Dad

Connie He's in bed –

Tom I'll go and get him up.

Connie You'll do no such thing –

Tom Labour's won – it's a bloody landslide, Mam – nobody expected this – hundred and forty odd seat majority –

Connie I know.

Tom That means we can – what do you mean you know?

Connie I know, I heard it on t' wireless.

Tom Well, have you told him?

Connie Not yet, leave him. He's in bed and I'm not having him disturbed.

Tom But he'll want to know.

Connie Don't you dare –

Tom What is it, Mam?

Connie You didn't see him when he came home. He was that bad he'd had to come off face.

Tom	Nobody told me.
Connie	He had to see under-manager.
Tom	Are they stopping him.
Connie	They've finally made him see a bit of sense. They're trying to look after him – so they've offered him the job as button man.
Tom	Bloody hell.
Connie	It's take it or leave it apparently. So, he's not best pleased.
Tom	No, I can imagine. He'll be away from so much dust though.
Connie	I've told him that. I've told him I'm glad. I've been dreading him coming home some days when you see the state of him. It's hurting his pride.
Tom	What's he said?
Connie	He's talking about losing all his mates, his union work, not to mention the money.
Tom	He doesn't have to worry about that now I'm back and earning.
Connie	He says you should be going off soon to make your own way in life. And he's right, you should.
Tom	I'm not going anywhere, Mam.
Connie	We both know that your Lizzie's got other ideas.
Tom	I'm not ready for that yet.
Connie	You should tell her that, Tom – I've seen how she looks at you.

Tom Whatever happens, Mam – I'll always look after you and Dad.

Connie You're a good lad, Tom. You always have been. The irony of it, eh? He's going to come down and find out he's got the one thing he's been wanting for the last thirty years – and it's the self-same day when they've chucked him on the bloody scrap heap.

Act One Scene 14

[Mason's Kitchen, it is 1946. We see the men of the house in preparation for the night shift. Connie brings in their snap and exits. The two men sit at opposite ends of the table dressing for work. They mirror each other's movements. First, the left boot on, then the right. Then they stand and adjust braces/waistcoat. Then they put on their jackets. Tom puts on his cap and picks Georges up from the table. He tries to put it on his father's head but George knocks his hand away, reels back and snatches the cap. He places it on his own head and glares at Tom in resentment. George puts on an overcoat and the two men leave the kitchen as if walking to work.

From the darkness, a section of the set becomes the pit bottom. We hear the loud industrial din of the mine at work. It is illuminated as if by the men's miner's cap lamps. We see Tom, in shirt sleeves using a chair as a piece of machinery drilling and turning the legs in to the coal face with tremendous effort. George sits in a chair. The standard lamp has become the "button" and he holds it across his knee. As Tom labours on George switches the light on and off to represent the pressing of the button to stop and start the belt. This is repeated to demonstrate the monotony of his new life until – SILENCE as the machinery stops.]

George   Time for a wet, lad.

Tom   Aye.

INTERVAL

Act Two Scene 1

[The Mason's sitting room. An early evening in December 1946.
George is snoozing in his chair.
Liz enters from outside. She is wearing her coat.
She tries not to disturb George but he wakes.]

Liz   Sorry – I didn't want to wake you up.

George   I wasn't asleep, I was just resting my eyes.

Liz   Right – I'm sorry – I knocked but you didn't hear me –

George   Don't worry lass, every bugger comes in here as if it's Liberty Hall.

Liz   Is Tom upstairs getting ready?

George   Ready for what?

Liz   We're going to the pictures. Second house.

George   I think there might have been a change of plan.

Liz   How do you mean?

George   He's gone to chapel with his mam.

Liz   Chapel?

George   Don't worry. He's not seen the light and signed the bloody pledge.

Liz   But why has he gone to the chapel?

George   They've had a burst pipe. Water everywhere according to reports. So, Tom's gone to try and sort summat out.

Liz   So, you've no idea what time he'll be back –

George There's no telling with a job like that.

Liz Oh.

George Cheer up, you can always go tomorrow.

Liz It's the last night tonight. It's a thriller we wanted to see – "Wanted for Murder."

George I bet you will be when you get your hands on our Tom.

Liz I'd better go then – *[She turns to go]*

George You can wait for him – if you want.

Liz How are you?

George I'm o'reight up to t' neck.

Liz Tom's worried about you –

George They all are – but there's no need for fuss. I keep telling 'em it's only a bad chest and –

Liz And – what?

George I've seen enough bad chests in my time – so I know what to expect.

Liz I'm sorry –

George Nay lass, tha don't have to be sorry.

Liz They're doing a good job at getting everything ready for Vesting Day.

George I know, three weeks to go.

Liz Yes.

George There'll be some bloody sore heads on t' morning after an' all.

Liz Some of the managers were in the office today

	saying they're worried for their jobs. They were talking about some closures. But they're going to try and keep the men on – transfer 'em to other pits.
George	Union'll look after the lads – like they always have.
Liz	Will they?
George	Oh aye –
Liz	I'm not so sure.
George	What do you mean?

[She shakes her head.]

	We've never talked much have we, me and you.
	You came round every day when our Tom was away and I don't think you said more than half a dozen words to me.
Liz	Well, it's hard to get a word in sometimes.
George	Aye I know, but there's more to it than that.
Liz	Well – I was scared –
George	Scared of me?
Liz	No –
George	You don't have to be frightened of me.
Liz	I wasn't frightened of you. I was scared to say the wrong thing.
George	You can say owt you want to me –
Liz	That's just it though – I can't – you see, whenever I'm here the talk always turns to the union –
George	It's important to this family – it's important to

	all on us –
Liz	I know that – but union didn't do my Dad any good did it?
George	So, that's why you were scared –
Liz	I didn't want to remind you I was Jack Adams' daughter.
George	I've no grudge against you – our fight was with your Dad because he was a –
Liz	He was a scab – you can say it you know. I've been hearing it for the last ten years.
George	Not from me. I wouldn't victimise the family of a sc – a strike breaker.
Liz	But there's plenty of your members who would – and they still do.
George	Well that's wrong. It's them as break the strikes they should go for, not their families.
Liz	Do you think, when you attack a scab, it doesn't upset his family?
George	When you work underground you can only work with them as you can trust – and no bugger could trust him – so he couldn't have carried on – not at Burnstone Colliery any road.
Liz	Not at any colliery – the union had him blacklisted.
George	Aye well, he brought it on himself –
Liz	Our Norman was a babe in arms. My Mam had only just had him and it'd left her badly. I was fourteen, I'd just started work but my wages were nothing. We were desperate. That's why he

	went back –
George	He could have come for help –
Liz	My Mam says he did – but he was turned away –
George	No love. That's not true. She's wrong. He didn't come for any help –
Liz	Are you sure –
George	I am. I was one of the union men he would have come to.
Liz	Well – I don't know who to believe. He was never the same man after they'd beaten him up and he'd lost his job.
George	The union doesn't condone violence –
Liz	No, but it turns a blind eye dun't it?
	And, you know how hard it is for a man who's been a collier all his life to turn his hand to owt else.
George	He did though, didn't he?
Liz	Working in a pickle factory with me and the other lasses – it was degrading for him.
George	I don't see why.
Liz	Would you have done it?

[He does not answer.]

Liz	As soon as he was offered the job as driver he jumped at chance. It got him out of the factory and away from Burnstone. Wagging tongues – pointing fingers. The trouble was, it took him away from us an all. Away from his wife and kids. He liked it. He liked the freedom. When he

went into the shops delivering he liked the women who worked there an all. And, when one of them decided she liked him – he never came back.

He never contacts my mam – or me.

George Look, I know tha't a good, decent, hard-working lass. And I don't want to fall out with thee.

I worked with thi Dad. I knew him before tha were born. He were always trouble.

Liz Whatever you say about him – and whatever he's done to us – he's still my Dad. And I'll not forget what union did to him.

George But, you need to understand a few things. He never turned up to vote for owt we were fighting for. There's a lot like him. They never work for owt but they benefit from what others get for 'em.

Liz He wasn't the only one.

George We came out on strike that time because six of our lads had been sacked for not obeying an order that would have put their lives at risk. We came out to support 'em get 'em re-instated. But him and a handful of others broke that strike and we were buggered. That's what happens if you don't stand together.

Liz Tom's told me all that. And I understand – but that doesn't make it easier – it doesn't make it fair on us.

George Life's not fair, lass. But if working men don't show solidarity they'll walk all over us if they can.

	I hope that working in them offices hasn't put you on the management side?
Liz	I'm not on anybody's side –
George	Our Tom won't put up with that.
Liz	What do you mean?
George	He's a union man – like me –
Liz	No he's not –
George	He's union through and through and he's proved it since he got back –
Liz	He's a union man – but he's not like you –
George	What does that mean?
Liz	Well – you, and the other men think that the unions always right and you don't listen to reason – you don't compromise – like you said, you think everything's a fight –
George	It always has been –
Liz	But don't you think we've had enough of fighting? You've got the government you've always wanted – you've got nationalisation – can't you stop being so – belligerent?
George	Belligerent! We need to be. We're trying to build a new bloody nation here.
Liz	A new Jerusalem in England's green and pleasant land?
George	Don't you mock that song.
Liz	I wasn't.
George	Them words were the inspiration that put fire in men's bellies after we came back from the Great

	War, when we were fighting to build that "land fit for heroes" they promised us. But we never got it, did we?
Liz	Some of it –
George	And the ruling classes are still determined to keep us down. They keep folk poor and blame them for their own poverty. And the working man accepts this shit because he doesn't know any better. But it can be different this time.
Liz	How?
George	They've woken up at last. They've realised that it's them as creates the wealth and that it can be shared out fairly.

I'm too old and buggered to fight on. We need good, young, strong union men, lads who can carry the flag, lads who can build a better future. Lads like our Tom. But not if you're going to turn him against it – |

[He starts to cough and becomes short of breath.]

Liz	I'm sorry – I didn't mean to upset you like this.
George	It'd take more than a young lass like thee to upset me.
Liz	I'm going.
George	Nay, sit thy sen down.
Liz	No, you're not up to it. I'll come back and talk to you when you're feeling better – but I'm telling you straight before I go. I loved your Tom before he went away. I waited for him to come home and, since he's been home this past two years, I love him even more. I'm going to

	marry him –
George	Does he know that?
Liz	Not yet. But he will. And when we do get wed nothing is ever going to come between us. Not you, not my Mam, or what my Dad did – and certainly not the Union.

Act Two Scene 2

[Vesting Day, 1ˢᵗ January 1947, outside the colliery gates.
George and Connie stand facing the pit ready for the unveiling of the sign. They are in winter clothes. They stand huddled against the cold in a tight line as if on a hill overlooking the proceedings.]

Tom   It looks like everybody in Burnstone's here.

Liz   They've got the brass band to come out for it.

George   I should think they have.

Connie   I'd have thought they'd be worn out after all the concerts they've played over Christmas.

George   I wish I'd got as much breath as them buggers.

Tom   It's not a very warm day for standing about.

Liz   It's coldest winter in living memory, Tom. What do you expect.

Connie   George, wrap that scarf round your neck a bit tighter.

George   I'm reight enough.

Tom   It's a grand turnout, Dad.

Liz   First of January 1947, history's been made and we're all here to see it.

George   Aye, I never thought I'd live to see the day; I still can't believe it's happening.

Tom   It's a new beginning is this, Dad.

George   I hope so son, I hope so.

Connie   You're not going to be a killjoy, are you George? Not today of all days.

George Oh no, I'm pleased as punch.

Connie You've a funny way of showing it.

George From now on it's the men who mine the coal who'll see the benefit of their hard labour instead of a few owners and shareholders.

Liz They were saying in the office that it won't make any difference to the average bloke.

Tom Not at first – it's going to be a massive job, – changing everything – it'll take time.

Liz Some of the men were telling me that they think they own the mines. And that all the profits will be going straight to them.

Connie They're going to be disappointed, then aren't they?

Tom They'd be pulling your leg. Although they're not very bright some of 'em.

George The unions told 'em straight – we're not taking over for our own greed. We'll be running it for the government we've put in. That means we're running it for the people.

Liz They're talking about all the machines they'll be bringing in. Saying that it'll put some men out of work.

Connie Perhaps it'll give some of the older miners a chance to retire now and put their feet up.

George Don't you two bloody start – not today.

Liz Hey look, they're going to unveil the new sign.

[We hear a few muffled, distant lines of the unveiling speech followed by applause.]

George What's it say? I can't see to read it all.

Tom "This Colliery Is Now Being Managed
By The National Coal Board,
On Behalf Of The People"

Act Two Scene 3

[The Mason's kitchen, a Sunday afternoon in late February 1947 George and Connie are dressed in winter clothes, George is wrapped in a blanket. They are sitting as close to the fire as possible.]

Connie Are you all right George?

George No, I'm perished – just like everybody else.

Connie Do you want some more tea?

George If I drink any more I shall be pissing tea.

Connie George – there's no need for that.

[Tom enters he is dressed in as many winter clothes as he can find. He carries a bag with bread and basic foods and a newspaper which he places in front of George.]

Tom Oh, bloody hell.

Connie Is it no better out there?

Tom It's a bit milder and there's a bit of a thaw but paths and t' roads are treacherous.

George I've never known a winter like this.

Connie Nobody has, they say it's the harshest winter for three hundred years.

Tom I've not been this cold since t' Norway landing when we ended up in the bloody North Sea.

Connie There's tea here, Tom.

George What's the news from the pit.

Tom They're saying that we've all to go in tomorrow. We've got to go on getting good output.

George   But even if you double production they won't be able to move it.

Connie   According to the wireless, entire country's ground to a standstill.

Tom   Well, if we can get in we've got to go – it's better to have some coal ready for when it can be moved than to sit and wait.

George   The cheeky bastards!

Connie   George Mason! I will not have that pit language in this house.

Tom   What's up, Dad?

George   This bloody paper, that's what's up. Has tha read this, Tom?

Connie   What does it say?

George   It's blaming every bugger in t' Labour Party and our union for the fuel crisis.

Tom   They're saying that NUM gave Mannie Shinwell bad forecasts and then he underestimated how bad this winter was going to be.

Connie   Nobody knew it was going to be this bad.

George   Look at bloody headline:
"SHIVER WITH SHINWELL."

Tom   Read on. It gets worse.

George   *[Reading]* "the government feared to take on the NUM, whose members' absentee rates have risen considerably since the pre-war period. Shinwell was warned in mid-October that a coal shortage was possible, but gambled on a mild winter to keep consumption low so that he

	would not have to risk a confrontation with the miners."
Connie	Is that true?
George	They're blaming the unions for an energy crisis that's all due to this bloody, rotten winter. But that's the Daily Mail for you. I don't know why tha's brought the fascist rag into this house.
Tom	It's only one they had.
George	Two months we've been nationalised and they're trying to destroy us already.
Tom	Dad, don't take this wrong way but – but you're not on t' face day in day out like you were.
George	Not through choice.
Tom	This article's a disgrace but it's right on one thing. Absenteeism's gone up. Even Jim Potts and t' other big union men are worried about it.
George	Well, why are they letting 'em get away with it?
Tom	A lot of the men are saying that they don't have to answer to the gaffers now that the pits belong to them.
George	Silly buggers.
Tom	This morning somebody's changed the colliery sign to "Managed by the National Coal Board on Behalf of the Miners."
George	I've told 'em they shouldn't be taking owt for granted.
Tom	You know as well as I do that if they start pulling too many strokes they're going to undo all the good work you blokes have done.

Connie   Well, what can they do to stop it.

Tom   We've got to educate men. Teach 'em that it's not like it was. It will be better, in time, but they can't just come and go as they please.

George   We've got a meeting on this Tuesday night. I need to talk to 'em, put 'em straight.

Connie   You're not fit to go anywhere, especially this weather.

George   They'll listen to me though –

Connie   There's others in the union besides you – what about our Tom why can't he stand in for you.

Tom   I don't know if they'd listen to me.

George   Make 'em listen. Connie – get me that writing pad and a pencil.

Act Two Scene 4

[We see George writing at the table whilst Tom addresses the Tuesday night Union meeting]

Tom My Dad wanted to come here to talk to you tonight but, as you know, he's badly so he's asked me to come and bring a couple of messages for you.

But I'm not just here to be a messenger boy for my Dad. I'm going to tell you what I think. There'll be some of you who'll be saying "what bloody right as he got to tell us what he thinks – he's only been back here for eighteen months."

Well – in one way, that does give me a right to give my opinion because I've been able to think about things from outside – most of you lads have spent the war grafting here every day, and that's summat you should all be proud of.

When you're in the army, in wartime, you spend half your time shitting yoursens in fear and other half being bored stiff. And when you are sat there with nowt to do, you think about home, the people, your town, your job. You think about what it's going to be like when you get back.

If anybody had told me then that it would have been like this I wouldn't have believed 'em.

My Dad, bless him, and a lot of the older blokes in this room have fought tooth and nail over the last thirty years to get what's been achieved.

We got Labour in with a big majority. And

they've kept every promise they made. On welfare, on a health service for next year that's going to be free to use and look after folk from cradle to grave. Great changes – for everybody.

But the best change for us is the Nationalisation of the coal industry.

It were never going to be the miracle that some were expecting.

But just stop for a minute and think what has been done. There were over a thousand collieries in this country run by eight hundred different companies. All run in their own sweet way.

Some have been grand, Burnstone's not so bad. Others are bloody awful, where men are still treated like they were a hundred year ago – like animals.

But Shinwell's done a bloody good job bringing them all together in such a short time. He's made some mistakes – bound to have – they're even blaming him for the bloody weather.

And you're not going to like this – but we're not helping the cause.

Nationalisation doesn't mean we own the pits. We only manage 'em, as that sign says, "On Behalf of the People" – they belong to everybody.

We can't come and go as we please. We don't have to be scared of management – all that finished in 1945. But we can't ignore 'em.

You see, now, it's not thousands of miners pitted against a few owners. Pits belong to the nation. Now we've all got to find ways of working together otherwise, mark my words, as soon as all this government investment starts to a show a profit, they'll use it as an excuse to take everything back into private hands.

Act Two Scene 5

[Late 1948, The Masons' kitchen
George is alone and asleep in his chair. He is very still.
Tom and Liz enter. They see George and are careful not to wake him.
Tom goes over to George. He listens for his breathing and, when
satisfied all is well, goes to put the kettle on the stove. George stirs and
wakes.]

Tom	Sorry, Dad. Did I wake you up?
George	No – I wasn't asleep – I was just resting my eyes.
Tom	Where's my Mam?
George	WVS or t' Chapel – I don't know – she did tell me as she went racing out. Where've you two been?
Liz	It were such a lovely day we decided to go up for a walk on Miller's Moor.
George	Aye, it'll be grand up there today.
Tom	What have you been up to?
George	Well I got up this morning and had a bit of breakfast sat in that chair. Then I read my paper sat in this one. Then your mam made me some dinner and I sat in that one again. Then I come back to this chair and sat here reading my paper again until I nodded off.
Liz	You've had a good rest then?
George	I've only been off for a week and I'm mooching about like a bear with a sore arse. I'm going back in Monday.

Liz   If t' doctor says two weeks off that's what you should have.

George   I thought I was bored working on the button but compared to this it's bloody exciting.

George   Does tha remember old Sam Bailey?

Tom   No.

George   Tha does – we called him Nelson – on account of him only having one eye.

Tom   Oh yes, did he retire while I was away?

George   No, he died at work – on the button.

Liz   That doesn't mean to say that's what's going to happen to –

George   They kept giving him two bells to stop the belt and nowt happened. Bloody coal were piling up – they thought he'd fallen asleep – he'd done it before. Anyway, when they went to wake him up they found him dead.

Liz   Poor man.

George   We all said he'd died of boredom. Sat there day in and day out wi' his one good eye trained on that button waiting to press it. What kind of job is that for a grown man?

Tom   It's an important job.

George   It's no life though, sat there all day thinking about things that tha could be doing.

[He takes a book from down the side of his chair]

Na then, what's this I've found in t' drawer?

Tom   Oh.

George	Deputy's manual.
Tom	Dad, I wasn't going to mention it yet but – Longmate called me in last week and offered me a chance to get my deputy's ticket.
George	Oh, did he? And what did tha tell him?
Tom	That I'd think about it.
George	But tha thought tha'd study t' handbook just in case?
Tom	Jack Hill lent me that when he found out.
George	So, Jack Hill knew afore me did he?
Tom	Whether I do it or not it'll be good knowledge to have.

[Long pause. Liz and Tom exchange glances. She prompts him to carry on speaking to his Dad.]

Look, Dad, I know you'll probably see it as joining management, and I'd be in a different union and all that, but its nearly two years since nationalisation, we've got three lots of managers – folk at head office in London, at area, at district levels and some on 'em haven't a bloody clue about mining. They said they need people helping to run things at pit level who know the job, people who might be able to work their way up – folk who've been born to it.

[George does not answer.]

Liz	It could be a big chance for him Mr Mason –
George	Is this your doing? Getting him in to management–
Liz	No, I –

George Getting him out of the union because if it is –

Tom Don't blame Liz. She's had no say in this. I make my own decisions and I think I'd make a better deputy than half the buggers you've worked under–

George I know all that –

Tom Well then –

George Do it.

Tom Eh?

George Do it.

Liz We thought you'd be dead against it.

George I would have been once. But not now. As soon as I saw this book I knew what tha were going to do.

Liz So all along –

George I had to be sure he weren't doing it for t' reight reasons not just for thee –

Go and be a deputy, son, and then if tha gets a chance to move up management ladder – take it.

Tom I never thought I'd hear you say that.

Liz Neither did I.

George I've got badly lass. And it must be all this bloody thinking and pondering I've been doing.

It's reight what they're telling you. It's no good having a bloody nationalised coal industry run by people who know bugger all about it. They need men of your generation who do understand it.

And look at me. All these year's on t' face working with these *[he shows his hands]* and not with this *[he taps his temple]* and what have I to show for it, eh?

A bad back and lungs full of shit. If tha's got a chance to better thi sen and not end up like this – take it.

Act Two Scene 6

[Tom stands under the standard lamp. He is studying his manual. He moves to a chair and begins to put on his boots to get ready for the night shift.

Connie and Liz enter. They are wearing their coats.]

Tom   How is he?

Connie   Not so good love, not so good.

Tom   Did you tell him why I couldn't come.

Liz   He knows you're working tonight.

Connie   He's wasn't expecting you to go.

Tom   I'll get up there tomorrow afternoon.

Connie   He's very tired, love. They're doing their best for him – hospitals been made lovely – it's spotless and I've never seen so many nurses.

Liz   At least he's being well looked after.

Connie   And it's not costing him a penny, so that's pleased him.

[Connie is tearful]

Tom   Hey come on, Mam – you know what he's like – stubborn as a mule. He'll not let this beat him.

Connie   He'll have no choice this time. I've spoken to the doctor – nice young man.

Tom   What's he said?

Connie   What we already knew – All they can do is dose him up with medicines and linctus to ease it a bit.

Liz	They said he could come home if there was somebody to nurse him.
Connie	I'll try and get him home next week.
Tom	It'll be a big strain on you, Mam.
Connie	Ay well, it's what we do love in't it?
	You're going to be late.
Tom	I know – Are you walking down as far as home with me, Liz?
Liz	No, I'm going to stay with your mam for a bit – if that's all right.
Connie	Course it is love.

[Tom exits]

	Are you all right love?
Liz	I'm just worried about Tom – I can see how upset he is about his Dad.
Connie	Don't fret. Tom'll look after himself. He's always been an old head on young shoulders.
	Is anything else troubling you?
Liz	No –
	Well –
Connie	If you want to tell me about the baby – I already know.
Liz	Tom said he wasn't going to say anything yet – he said that you had enough on your plate.
Connie	Our Tom's not breathed a word – he didn't have to –
Liz	Does it show?

Connie	No love – but when you've seen as many pregnancies as I have you know all the signs.
Liz	I'm sorry –
Connie	Don't be sorry – don't be sorry for giving me my first grandchild.
Liz	I thought you'd be angry. You being chapel and all.
Connie	If I were to start condemning you for that I'd be a hypocrite.
Liz	What do you mean?
Connie	We all have secrets love.
	When I married George, I was expecting our Judd – I was nearly four months gone.
Liz	I didn't know –
Connie	Not many do – not even Tom.
	When I told my father, he disowned me and threw me out – he was a Methodist lay preacher and men like him didn't tolerate sin.
	But George's family, they took me in. Oh, they weren't Christians – but they showed us all the Christian charity anybody could want.
	What's your Mam said?
Liz	She doesn't know – I daren't tell her – she'll go mad.
Connie	You must tell her love, straight away.
Liz	She'll throw me out –
Connie	Well, if she does I've got a spare bed.
	Have you and our Tom made any plans.

Liz Tom wants us to go to the registry office and do it all quick and quiet and he's asking at the pit for a house – now that the Coal Board own all the old tied houses – he thought we might get one of those –

Connie You don't want to live down in the rows do you? Those houses are awful.

Liz No, I don't, but Tom says we have to start somewhere and when they've finished building all the new ones they've promised we'll apply for one of them.

Connie And what about you, Liz?

Liz What do you mean.

Connie Well, so far I've heard a lot about what our Tom wants – what do you want?

Liz I don't know –

[She begins to cry. Connie goes to comfort her.]

Connie Hey, come on now love.

Liz I'm sorry – I'm all mixed up – I don't know what I want –

Connie I'm not surprised.

Liz It's just that everything's seemed to be going so well – since Tom came back – I've been so happy – I've got a good job – been able to treat our Norman – afford nice things like it was before my Dad went – and now it's all going to change. I'm going to have to leave 'em – leave my job – they'll be worse off and so will I. We thought we'd been so careful because we had made such plans.

Connie When mother nature takes over love all your plans go out of the window.

Liz But I wanted to have some savings – I wanted our life to be different to my Mam's – and yours and half the lasses round here – just one big struggle all the time.

I don't know if I want this baby.

Connie It's a big thing, having your first child. But there's a world of difference now to when I had my two. Especially now – look at that hospital that's going to be there for you. When I had mine, I had 'em at home and the woman from four doors down was the local midwife.

Liz Oh, don't.

Connie Look, your lives will be different.

Liz Do you think so?

Connie Our Tom's working hard to get on in his job. When he gets his deputy's papers he'll have a wage coming in every week come rain or shine. And a job for life. That's more than George could ever guarantee to me. Our Tom's a good lad and I know in my heart that he'll look after you – and the baby.

Liz I know – I'm not worried about Tom – but my Mam –

Connie Listen, just you point out to her that you and our Tom were sweethearts before he went away, that you waited for him for five years and that you've seen each other practically every day for the past three since he got back – eight years? I reckon its high time he married you – all this bairn's done is given him the kick up the backside he needed.

Look, you dry your eyes and then go home and tell your Mam what's happened as calm as you can. Now I'm not going to interfere, but if she wants to come round and talk about what we can both do to help you – she knows where I live.

[Tom bursts in]

Tom　　Mam, Mam –

Connie　Tommy what's a matter –

Tom　　It's my Dad – he's had a turn for the worse – they stopped me at gate – we've got to go to the infirmary now –

Connie　Oh my Lord – How are we going to get there?

Tom　　Jim Potts – he's brought me home – he's taking us – he's waiting outside with his car – quick as you can –

Act Two Scene 7

[Connie is dressed in black after the funeral. She holds a floral china cup and saucer. She taps the side of the cup with a spoon to get our attention.]

Connie Can I have your attention everybody? Just for a few moments – because I'd just like to say a few words – a few words of thank-yous.

First of all, thank you to the co-op and the staff for a lovely tea. And thank you to all of you for coming here to give George a wonderful send off. He'd have been very proud to see so many people who he's worked with – and worked for – over the years, come to pay your respects.

That's a big word isn't it – respect?

George never wanted much out of life. Not for himself anyway. He wasn't always an easy man to deal with and nobody knows that more than me. When he was at his most determined and stubborn he could be impossible. But these faults turned into virtues in his work.

They made him a fighter. They made him fight for what he believed in. Fight for his workmates and friends. Fight for his family.

And when I look around this room today and I see men who've worked alongside him underground for years, I see a generation of fighters. I see men like George who've worked their lives away to provide a better future for the next generation.

Some of that next generation went away to fight

for us in a different way – some didn't come home. And after we lost our Judd – well – George was never the same man again' but the fight didn't go out of him – he was still determined that the world should be a better place for working people.

In the early days a lot of us – including me – used to laugh at George – you called him "Lenin." You managers called him a communist agitator.

Maybe he was – I don't know – but what I do know is that he never let a single one of you down, and he might have used a lot of words, but he meant every single one of them.

That's his legacy. That's what earned him his respect.

Raise your glasses please – to George Mason.

Epilogue

Tom Down there is my town.
Burnstone.
Where I grew up, where I came home to eight years ago.

George Where I worked, where I earned our living.

Connie Where I brought up a family, where I made a home.

Liz Where I grew up, where I fell in love, where I waited.

Tom That's my town, Burnstone. A town of two thousand souls: every one of them connected to what lays beneath it – coal.
There's been a pit here since 1756 –

George It's not a pit son, a pit's just a hole in the ground. It's a mine, a coal mine.

Tom There's been a mine here since 1756 – without it there wouldn't be a town. Our lives depend on it.

George It's taken a good few lives an all.

Tom A town on the side of the Pennines.

George On the reight side of the Pennines.

Tom In this valley carved out millions of years ago, the town grew. First in the valley bottom, but now the newer cottages and houses, their grey stone hewn from the Pennine rock, cling to the hillsides as if their lives depend on it.
And at the bottom end of the valley, Burnstone

	Colliery, its headgear and its winding wheel dominating the landscape.
Liz	And now the town's over-spilled the valley rim like a pot boiling over. It's poured on to Millers Moor, they've built The Millers Moor Estate, where we live.
George	It's a bloody shame.
Connie	It's a wonderful place. Avenues of houses with three bedrooms, bathrooms and gardens back and front.
Liz	Gardens where my two children can play in the fresh air. Avenues where we've hung the bunting and put up the tables for the Coronation.
Tom	These hills are made for walking in.
Liz	Look at that beautiful view.
Connie	Breathe in that fresh air.
George	The town below, like an ugly picture in a beautiful frame.
Liz	And I'm living closer to nature up here than I ever thought I would.
George	Look at that hawk soaring and gliding and diving for a kill.
Connie	It's where we have long sunny days, family picnics.
Liz	It's where we hold hands, where we make plans.
Connie	We're lucky – I'm lucky – to live with my lovely family. My two grandchildren, playing, laughing, running through the fresh, stiff breezes.

Tom	Then I have to go back down the valley, sometimes at four in the morning – an hour before my lads start their shift – I'm a deputy.

Liz	See you later love.

Connie	I hope he's safe.

George	He'll be reight!

Tom	Course I'll be reight, Dad! We'll all be reight!

It's not like in your day. We've moved on. More machines coming in every month, big uns, wider roadways, better ventilation. More safety regulations than I can keep pace with.

You'd be proud.

We didn't destroy what had been built with your generation's sweat and muscle. Instead we've built on it. In the last six years built an industry that's going to fuel this country for ever and a day – an industry that looks after the men who work in it and looks after the families who depend on them.

We're building an industry that'll go on working forever, cutting coal –

On Behalf of the People.

THE END

About the Author

Ray Castleton got into acting and writing after graduating from the University of Leeds in 2011 at the tender age of 63. His play *Chicken Soup* which he co-wrote with Kieran Knowles was a sell-out at The Crucible Theatre. He has had various acting roles in theatre and on TV.

If you enjoyed reading this play, it would be appreciated if you could write a review of the book on Amazon or Goodreads or whichever online sites you use: just a line or two would be great. Word of mouth is so important when you've not got a marketing department and financial backing behind you. Thanks!

Performance Licence

Because a lot of graft went into producing this work it is copyrighted. (Well, you wouldn't work for free would you? Sadly, like everyone else, writers have bills to pay.)

It would be great to see other public performances of the work, so please apply for a licence. This is needed for any public performance, including readings and excerpts, irrespective of whether you charge for tickets or not. A licence is also needed to reproduce the text in whole or in part, in any format.

To apply for a licence please contact: Ray Castleton (raycastleton@hotmail.com). Thanks for respecting the author's hard work.

www.ingramcontent.com/pod-product-compliance
Lightning Source LLC
Chambersburg PA
CBHW061803070526
44586CB00023B/2688